Practical Wisdom

VOLUME I

Quotes and Comments That Inspire, Enlighten, and Entertain

Rick Ott

Ocean View Communications
A division of Symmetric Systems, Inc
www.oceanviewcommunications.com

Written by: Rick Ott
Edited by: Cherry Cézanne
Cover photo: Rick Ott. (Indian Field Creek, Williamsburg, Virginia, U.S.A.)
Cover art: Ott & Associates

Printed in the United States of America

ISBN: 978-0-9663491-7-7

Contents

Featured Person Listed by Page Number

Continued . . .

Contents (continued)

*You only grow by coming
to the end of something
and the beginning of
something else.*

• John Irving

John Irving is an American novelist and screenwriter.

I can recall the sad, empty feeling of the last days of high school . . . saying goodbye to the people and the environment that had been a large part of my life. Then college started and it was a whole new environment with a whole new bunch of friends. Same thing happened as my college days ended. The sadness of letting go, followed by the excitement of a new life.

Seems this ending-of-something/beginning-of-something-else cycle just keeps repeating as I go — and grow — through life.

Perhaps something in your life is ending right now. Maybe it's a job or project. Maybe it's your home or life-style. Maybe someone special is gone. Keep in mind, the sadness of the end will be supplanted by the happiness of the new, in time. And the happiness can come quicker if you realize that this transition is really growth . . . a good thing.

It's true that some ending-to-beginning transitions you experience may be negative growth; a setback. When this happens, remind yourself of these two truths:

1. **Growth, or progress, is never a straight line upward.** Growth is more like a sawtooth line composed of small upward, downward, and level movements. Over greater lengths of time, it's a upward progression, however.

2. **A setback is only temporary,** provided you are willing to let go of it and keep moving forward regardless. A setback can actually be a springboard for even greater, faster success if you are willing to accept this belief and continue putting forth effort.

The more you watch TV,
the less you're going to accomplish.

• Ted Turner

Ted Turner is the founder of cable networks CNN, TBS, and TCM.

The three best things about television:
1. You can learn a little about a lot of different things. (I never knew some turtles can live over two hundred years until I saw one of these old guys on Animal Planet.)
2. You can be entertained on demand.
3. It's a great source of company when you're alone.

The worst thing about television: It chews up a whole lot of your time.

It's not just television. As we have come to find out, smart phones, the internet, and video games can be just as great a time burner.

Since we only have one life to live, and a relatively short one at that (at least compared to some turtles), may I suggest you turn off the TV, put down the smart phone, or disengage from the video games for a while and instead engage in some productive endeavor?

Think of something you've accomplished, however big or small. Did it happen with the television off? With the smart phone out of your hands? With the video game console off? More than likely, the answer is yes to all of the above.

Here's how to "find" one more hour each day, thirty more hours each month, one extra month each year: turn off the electronic distractions. One more thing: It helps if you spend less time sitting and more time moving.

Choose a job you love,
and you'll never have to work
a day in your life.

• Confucius

❧

Confucius was a Chinese teacher and philosopher who lived from 551-479 BC.

The theory is: If you really love what you do, it won't seem like work. The practicality of it is: There will be a whole lot of times when your chosen profession seems like work, even distasteful drudgery.

My Thrill Immunity theory states that you will become immune to the thrill of whatever you spend a lot of time with. So, the more time you spend with the job you love, the more apathetic, listless, burned out, you can become.

It doesn't have to see this way. It can be the way Confucius suggests, where you really do feel excited about your job most of the time. Here's how to make that happen and avoid Thrill Immunity:

- **Step back and self-assess your disposition.** Do you find yourself lacking interest, thrill, or excitement while on the job? Do you find yourself even resenting the demands of the job? The funny thing about Thrill Immunity is that we usually don't realize it's affecting us until we hit bottom. I'm asking you to realize it now — before it drags you closer to the bottom.
- **Get a new perspective.** Spend a little time thinking about (a) what it might be like having to do a job you really hate, (b) all those other people who would love to have the job you have, and (c) given the alternatives, how fortunate you are to have the job you do.

Every profession — even those considered glamorous or exciting — has its down-and-dirty aspects, which one will naturally experience when one is deeply involved. The key is to realize you actually do love your job, warts and all. Only then will you cease "working".

There's no half speed.
You either go all the way
or you don't go at all.

• Jimmy Johnson

Jimmy Johnson is a former NFL and college football coach and current NFL broadcaster.

From a football coach's perspective, you might think Jimmy is referring to football players literally running, blocking, tackling with vigor. That can certainly be the case at times. There are other times, however, in football and in life, when one's physical movement is not going to be full throttle, for a variety of reasons.

What Jimmy is really referring to is one's level of commitment or determination, which should be all the way on to achieve results.

Whenever you find yourself tentative or hesitant, it's okay to step back and reassess. Is this really something you should be doing? If your answer is yes, then re-commit and jump back in there. Give it everything you've got.

One summer I was with a small group of people attending a local fair. As the sun set and the main concert was to start, we found ourselves outside the big tent questioning whether we should invest more time and money in this outing by attending the concert. Someone said they heard the performer was good; someone else said the performer wasn't very good. Someone else said they didn't care one way or the other. Recalling Jimmy Johnson's statement, I said "We came here to have a good time. If we're not going to take in the entire show, then we shouldn't have come in the first place." It turned out to be an exceptional performance, and everyone had a great time.

Check your level of commitment and/or determination. Fire it up. Show what you can do.

Do what you love,
and the money will come.
Love what you do,
and the money will come.

• Louise Hay

Louise Hay is a writer and publisher.

There are both spiritual and practical reasons why doing what you love — or loving what you do — will bring you money.

From the spiritual standpoint: You have been given some special talent, ability, aptitude, or skill. When you use this gift in ways that better mankind, the immutable law of reciprocation provides you with rich rewards, including money.

From the practical standpoint: It stands to reason that you will spend more time and effort, with contagious enthusiasm, doing something that you love doing. That being the case, you will get really good at it. You will surpass those that don't have your level of skill and enthusiasm. The marketplace tends to pay — sometimes really well — those who have demonstrated a high level of proficiency at something. Therefore your services are in demand and the money flows.

What if you're doing something you love and money is not coming? In order for the money spigot to open, you need three important elements in addition to a love for your work.

1. You need to be really good at it.
2. You need to do it longer than you have been. No one, despite illusions to the contrary, is an overnight success.
3. You need higher visibility or exposure. Lots of people need to know about you and the exceptional work you're doing.

Being alone and out of love
is forty-nine percent good
and fifty-one percent bad.
Being with someone and in love
is fifty-one percent good
and forty-nine percent bad.

• James Curtis Gorman, III

JCGIII is a former radio personality and advertising executive,
and current aviation aficionado.

What's perhaps the biggest detriment to your love life? Expecting your happiness level to skyrocket by falling in love and getting married. Even those who acknowledge that "relationships take effort" still seem to fall into the trap of expecting their happiness level to shoot up dramatically when they get into a relationship.

In truth, the love and marriage balance sheet has, on one side: attraction, stimulation, companionship, help, support, and caring. And on the other side: tolerance, compromise, disagreement, argument, anger, and disappointment. Both sides weigh out pretty much even.

For better or worse, JCGIII's observation may be reality. Therefore, it's probably a good idea to realize that love and marriage is only going to raise your happiness level one tiny amount. Prepare for that outcome.

"Wait a minute," you say. "My marriage is going great and I'm really happy!"

My response would be either . . .

    (a) In time — when the euphoria wears off — things will revert back to even. Or . . .

    (b) You and your spouse are in the one-tenth of one-percent that do seem to live in perpetual euphoria. You are very fortunate.

*The longer we dwell on our misfortunes,
the greater is their power to harm us.*

• Voltaire

❧

Voltaire was a French philosopher and writer who lived from 1694 to 1778.

During my early college years, I worked as a disc jockey on the campus radio station. Having no prior on-air experience, I made my share of mistakes. I eventually noticed that when I dwelled upon a mistake I had just made, such as allowing too much "dead air" between a jingle and song, I subsequently made even more mistakes during the remainder of my airshift that day. One mistake seemed to trigger an avalanche of mistakes, with me feeling progressively worse with each one.

I decided the best way to handle a mistake is to immediately forget that I had made it. That way, it wouldn't do any further damage. That way, it wouldn't prevent me from performing exceptionally for the remainder of my airshift. That way, I would render the mistake inconsequential.

I literally trained my brain to immediately forget each mistake I made, and it worked. My overall performance, and my disposition, improved remarkably. To this day, I still exercise my mistake-forgetting skill to remain free of the poisonous effects of dwelling on misfortune.

You can develop this skill also. Immediately upon making a mistake or suffering a misfortune, force your attention onto something new that is happening or is about to happen, and away from what just happened. You must do this until it becomes programmed into your subconscious, after which it will happen automatically.

The result should be a noticeable improvement in your performance, and an equal improvement in the quality of your life and in the lives of people you affect.

Since you have to think anyway,
you may as well think big.

• Donald Trump

Donald Trump is an entrepreneur and was elected President of the United States in 2016.

Thinking big can be rewarding. Let me add this, however: Thinking big is a great first step, but you must also act in a big way. Donald Trump doesn't just think big — he takes action, on a continual basis, to make those big ideas happen.

It is really a combination of two thing — big thinking and continual action — that builds empires. One without the other doesn't build much at all.

*Talent is of no value
unless recognized by others.*

• George Bernard Shaw

❧

George Bernard Shaw was an Irish playwright who lived from 1856 to 1950.

If you want to use your talent to make a living, you need mass exposure.

It doesn't matter what your talent is, or how much of it you have. What does matter is how many people become exposed to your talent. That's because very few people, relative to the entire population, will be able to recognize your talent. And only a minuscule percent of those that do will be in a position to help you out in some way.

When you examine the careers of famous people who live by their talent, you discover three common occurrences:

1. They had to endure dozens — or perhaps hundreds or even thousands — of people who either did not recognize their talent or were in no position to do anything about it even if they did recognize it.
2. They only needed the recognition and support of one person. But, this person had to be in a position to hire them, promote them, or manage their career in a big way.
3. They needed recognition and support by some contingent of the population at large. Fans, voters, consumers, and the like.

Nothing's impossible.
Impossible just takes a couple
extra phone calls.

• Michael J. Fox

❧

Michael J. Fox is a television and movie actor.

First, choose carefully which endeavors really are worth pursuing. Since you have limited resources (no one has unlimited time, talent, or money), and since you can't keep calling upon the same few friends to help you with ever possible venture or project that interests you, be selective.

Then, once you have a clear objective in your sights, and a passion for attaining it, talk to lots of people. There is someone somewhere that would love to help you do the "impossible," especially when there's something in it for them.

*The world will stand in line
behind you and support you —
but only if you tell the world
what you want to accomplish.*

• Gloria Gault Geary

Gloria Gault Geary is a professional speaker and real estate agent.

If you're not getting the support you think you deserve, from family, friends, colleagues, or the world at large, perhaps it's because people have no idea what it is you're trying to accomplish.

When you clearly articulate exactly what it is you're going for, and demonstrate a high level of desire and determination, a funny thing happens. People around you get excited. They instinctively understand the power of determination, and are more likely to cheer you on or even become involved in some way. (Or at least the get out of the way.)

If you want someone in particular to support you, you need to tell that person exactly what you're attempting to accomplish. You may also have to instruct them on *how* to support you. Tell them precisely what you would like them to say or do. Once they get the hang of it, their support will grow.

There's another aspect of this that you need to be aware of and prepare for. When you announce your intentions in an effort to gain support, you simultaneously nurture an opposing element. Some people may react with resentment, jealousy, or disbelief. Although such reaction is usually inappropriate and unfortunate, it is common. Don't let the detractors catch you by surprise, and don't let them discourage you. You and your supporters simply have to ignore the negative energy and press on regardless.

*You are having more fun
than you think you are.
These are great days!*

• Rick Ott

Your brain tends to discount pleasurable experiences and heighten unpleasant experiences at the time they're happening. Your brain will then do the opposite when recalling past experiences — heightening the pleasurable and softening the unpleasurable.

Observe how some people act when on vacations. They're with family or friends — the people most important in their lives. They're in a beautiful setting, surrounded by great weather, with interesting things to see, and exciting things to do. Yet you'll see them bitching, moaning, complaining almost non-stop. They're so manipulated by the brain's immediate tendency to discount the pleasurable and heighten the displeasurable that they fail to realize they're actually drenched in fun. Then, years later, they'll think back to that time and say "gee, that was fun!" Have you ever behaved similarly?

Ten years from now you will look back on today with great fondness. You'll remember the people, places, and experiences that made life fun back then (which is really now).

The key is to value each day of your life as it's happening, not strictly in retrospect. Value all your daily experiences, from the ordinary to the extraordinary. Realize that throughout most of it, you are having fun.

Happiness consists more in small conveniences or pleasures that occur every day, than in great pieces of good fortune that happen but seldom to a man in the course of his life.

• Benjamin Franklin

Benjamin Franklin was a writer, publisher, inventor, statesman, and one of the founding fathers of the United States of America. He lived from 1705 to 1788.

Have you ever said "If only (insert some desired occurrence) happened, I'd be happy"? That type of statement usually leads to either (a) the occurrence never happens and you go through life unhappy, or (b) the occurrence does happen and you become happy for a short time, but lapse back into unhappiness shortly thereafter.

Don't make your happiness contingent upon occurrences, especially big ones. Doing so sets you up for unnecessary, undeserving misery. Instead, decide that you are happy starting right now and continuing throughout the remainder of your life.

This doesn't mean you are always content or aren't wanting for more. Displaying ambition and effort, aimed at bettering yourself and others, is almost always appropriate. Just strive from a position of happiness rather than from a position of unhappiness.

There is no big bang.
It's a series of baby steps
that produces results.

• Wolf J. Rinke

❧

Wolf J. Rinke is a professional speaker and author.

Everything you do, however big or small, has a positive effect in combination with everything else you do. But any one thing you do, however big or small, has little to no effect by itself.

It's like building a brick wall. Each brick, in combination with all the others, produces a large, strong wall. But a single brick by itself doesn't do much of anything. (Yes, there is an exception. A single act can have a monumental, lasting effect if it's incredibly spectacular or incredibly horrific.)

The key word is *series*. It's a series of baby steps that gets you from where you are to where you want to be. Which is how that big, strong wall came to be. Each brick was laid one at a time, in succession, over time. And that's exactly how you are going to accomplish things — once step at a time, over time.

(See related quote, next page.)

Everyone I know who got a big break
[subsequently] took a big fall.
It's really a series of small breaks
[that leads to success].

• Jay Leno

❧

Jay Leno is a comedian and television personality.

Here's the problem with the big break: It's too slow to arrive and too quick to dissipate. Not to mention the fact that it's too difficult to engineer.

You need only look to Hollywood to see that the big break isn't all it's cracked up to be. Every day some aspiring actor lands a plum part in a television show or movie, only to fade back into oblivion shortly thereafter.

Of course, if a big break happens to come your way, take it. You have every right to be excited and appreciative of your good fortune. Realize, however, that the effects of the big break will be fleeting. You'll need to continually follow up with a series of small breaks (which are engineerable) to keep success alive and growing.

We are what we repeatedly do.
Excellence, then, is not
an act, but a habit.

• Aristotle

Aristotle was a Greek philosopher and writer. He lived from 384 to 322 B.C.

I hired a contractor to make some repairs to my house and deck. The three-man crew did a great job, and they did it fast. They're good at this type of work because they do it every day. Although I enjoy home improvement work and could have done some of it myself, I wouldn't have done as good a job — and it would have taken me ten times as long.

Look at someone who does something really well, and you'll see that they owe a lot of their success to habit. They simply do it all the time.

What about talent, or skill, you ask? Could it be those contractors have a particular talent or skill that makes them good at home improvement work? Sure, talent, natural ability, and skill are all part of the success equation. But to make your talent useful, you have to use it often. Raw talent turns into effective skill through repeated learning and doing — the habit.

If you want to develop some new skill, just start doing it. Allow yourself time to be lousy at first; that's to be expected. In time, as you repeatedly learn and do, your habit is formed, your skill level rises, and your successes are ever greater.

*There isn't a Miss Right.
There are twelve-thousand Miss Rights,
and it's all timing.*

• Matthew Perry

Matthew Perry is a television and movie actor.

Opportunity is abundant, yet it is mysterious. It often disguises itself as misfortune, and prefers a quiet approach rather than a loud entrance. It is also fluid. Various opportunities come and go — entering your arena for a moment, then quickly slipping away. Only to be followed by a different but also fleeting opportunity some time later. And another after that.

Many times we fail to recognize opportunity when it arrives, or act upon it in time. Why? Because our attention or interest is elsewhere. In short, our timing was off.

You could meet the person of your dreams this evening, but if he or she doesn't "see" the opportunity you bring, nothing will happen. And haven't there been times in your life that, in retrospect, you now realize someone saw the possibility in you — but your mind was somewhere else at the time? They may have even called out to you in some obvious way (lo and behold, sometimes opportunity does hit you over the head) yet you failed to "see" that which could have been.

Recognizing opportunity is only one variable. Timing is actually composed many variables, most of which are out of your control. I refer to all the uncontrollable variables collectively as the "forces of the universe." And make no mistake about it, the forces of the universe run the agenda.

You can, however, tilt the odds in your favor by putting yourself in position more often. If you want to meet Miss Right or Mister Right, you need to connect with more people. Mathematical odds and timing go and in hand. To be the beneficiary of good timing more often, put yourself in position more often.

*Everything comes to him who
hustles while he waits.*

• Thomas Edison

Thomas Edison was an inventor who lived from 1847 to 1931.

To make things happen, you've got to have lots of irons in the fire. Hustling means putting a constant supply of new irons in the fire while others are heating up or burning out.

Instead of waiting for the payoff, spend your time heating new irons.

(See related quote, next page.)

There is no substitute for hustle,
and it takes no talent to hustle.

• Matt Millen

❧

Matt Millen is an NFL executive and broadcaster.

Talent is one thing, hustle another. It helps if you have both. But if you had to choose between them, which would you take?

Before you answer, consider this: I've known many talented people who can't seem to get anywhere for any length of time. I've also known other low-talent or no-talent people who hustle their way to admirable success. My conclusion is that hustle outweighs talent. What's yours?

There's really good news here. First of all, you don't need any talent to become highly successful if you're willing to hustle. Secondly, if you do have some talent, and hustle on top of that, you're headed for the top as long as you sustain your effort.

*No one ever lost credibility
by being interesting.*

• Tom Antion

❧

Tom Antion is a professional speaker, author, and internet marketing expert.

Here's how to be interesting in conversation:
- **Listen intently.** Pay attention to what the other person is saying and bounce off of that.
- **Ask good questions.** If you're listening intently, good questions will automatically come to you.
- **Focus the conversation on the other person(s)** rather than on yourself.
- **Look into the other person's eyes,** not around the room.

Here's how to be interesting when you write an article or deliver a speech:
- **Be relevant.** Is what you're saying relevant to the audience at this point in time?
- **Inform.** Tell them something they don't already know. This doesn't mean you are expected to break news, but it does mean your interpretation, organization, or application of the material is a new, useful twist.
- **Be concise.** Use as few words as possible to make your point.
- **Entertain a little.** Or entertain a lot if you're good at it. Humor and storytelling are the two most powerful ways to entertain in a speech or in prose.

Also, realize that you are not interesting when you spread gossip, despite the possible illusion to the contrary. Telling tales that hurt people — even if they're true — always sheds bad light upon the gossiper, and ratchets his or her credibility way down.

Sometimes long-term balance requires short-term imbalance.

• Mark Sanborn

❧

Mark Sanborn is a professional speaker and author.

Perhaps you are putting in long hours at your job or in school, or both. Perhaps you aren't spending as much time with your family, or your hobby, as you would like. There may be times in your life when that will happen. In the short run, periods of imbalance may be beneficial.

However, if others — such as your parents, spouse, or children — are making sacrifices to accommodate your imbalance, then they should share in the rewards your imbalanced endeavors eventually produce. An example would be the late Sam Walton, the founder of Walmart. In the early day of the company, Sam worked long hours, often away from his family. But when the company took off and matured, Sam got to spend more time with his family. And he left them millions to boot. The short-term imbalance certainly paid off for everyone.

Like many things that decrease in value when engaged in excessively, imbalance pays off only when it occurs in short intervals. When you start to feel overworked or perpetually stressed, you know it's time to balance things out in the other direction for a while.

*If one advances confidently
in the direction of his dreams,
and endeavors to live the life
which he has imanged,
he will meet with a success
unexpected in common hours.*

• Henry David Thoreau

❧

Henry David Thoreau was a poet and philosopher who lived from 1817 to 1862.

First, you've got to dream or imagine something different than what already exists. Visualize in your mind the type of life you would like and see yourself in that life.

Then, start acting like you're there now. Don't wait for something to happen or for someone to bless your wishes. Don't wait for financial wherewithal. Just start, regardless of your current circumstances.

As you advance, amazing things start to happen. Pathways that appeared blocked before now open up. The money you need materializes. People in position to help do help. Supporters grow.

I'm not saying it becomes easy. Nothing of any value comes easy. But as you advance, doors do open and hurdles become hurdleable.

The key is to keep moving in the direction of your dreams. When you do, you'll be amazed at what you accomplish.

The Street wanted to hear our dreams and aspirations. They'd hear me speak of things such as reaching a thousand stores or having stock valued at $100 or more. I lived in the future.

• Bernie Marcus

Bernie Marcus is cofounder of The Home Depot.

Bernie's dream was a nationwide chain of huge home improvement stores, not just one or two small ones. Despite tremendous resistance from both inside and outside the industry, he and Arthur Blank founded The Home Depot anyway. They went ahead and created what they envisioned, even though they had too few resources and too much opposition.

Steve Jobs and Steve Wozniak did the same thing when they started Apple Computer. They originally pitched their idea for a personal computer to Atari and then to Hewlett-Packard, and were turned down by both. (HP not only said no, but told them "We don't need you. You guys haven't been through college yet.") So the two Steves did it anyway, on their own.

The idea is to forge ahead, whatever the circumstances.

I decided to operate the same way. One of my aspirations (I have several) was to not only write books but to own and operate a publishing company. This book that you are reading right now was once a mere idea. Then I put in the time writing it and graphically laying it out. Then I started Ocean View Communications, a publishing company. (I used to live on Ocean View Avenue in Norfolk, Virginia. Thought it was a nice name.) I learned as I went, and it all worked out.

If we won every game we played,
it wouldn't be any fun.

• Brett Favre

Brett Favre is a former quarterback who played for 20 years in the NFL.

Losing from time to time, whether it be in sports, business, investing, or love, is a normal, natural occurrence. More than likely, you will lose a number of times throughout your lifetime.

You will also win a number of times. In fact, your wins will outweigh your loses by a significant margin, provided you don't allow your loses to destroy you along the way.

Here are three ways to reduce the negative effects of a loss:

1. **Remind yourself that if you won all the time, you'd be unchallenged, unfulfilled, and unmotivated.** If you won all the time, victory would hold no discernible thrill.

2. **Don't panic.** I have seen many instances when someone turned a minor setback into a major debacle, including managers and owners who ruined their own companies by overreacting. Violent response usually fuels a decline; calm response abates a decline.

3. **Maintain the course.** Yes, some changes may be in order. But if you still believe in your objectives and your ability to achieve them, stay the course even when the journey gets bumpy.

*Often an idea would occur to me
which seemed to have force. Such things
often come in a kind of intuitive way
more clearly than if one were to
deliberately reason them out.*

• Abraham Lincoln

Abraham Lincoln was the 16th President of the United States.

Here's why you should trust your instincts or intuition:
1. **There are a lot more brain cells at work guiding your intuition than are at work when you consciously reason.** Your genetic makeup, all your past experiences, and every bit of information about the present environment or situation, all combine to produce intuitive feelings or ideas.
2. **Intuition is not the same as emotion.** Your intuition can be very logical, rational, practical.
3. **If you go against your intuition and instead follow your reasoning (at times when the two are in conflict), you'll most likely regret it sooner or later.** If you follow your instincts instead of your reasoning, you'll be glad you did in the end.
4. **The most stressed, troubled people are those that have not resolved the inherent conflict that can exist between their intuition and their reasoning.** They try to reason everything out — constantly fighting their intuition — and thus live very unhappy lives.

One big exception: When you feel a sudden wave of anger, disappointment, jealousy, or any other negative emotion, your instinctive reaction might be to immediately lash out at others. You've heard it said before: count to ten before speaking; call a time-out on yourself; sleep on it. Your intuition will give you a much better course of action when you give it time to (subconsciously) work on the problem.

The other big exception: Your intuition need not rule in every situation. Sometimes, you are wise to defer to another person's intuition, if you feel theirs is stronger than your own, in a particular instance.

If you're not feeling tinges of
embarrassment or humiliation
from time to time,
you're not taking enough action.

• Rick Ott

"Taking action" is really composed of three sub-actions:

1. **Talking to people.**
2. **Committing yourself.**
3. **Engaging in physical movement.**

Yes, while taking these three sub-actions you automatically increase your vulnerability to a little embarassment or humiliation. A willingness to accept some of this discomfort puts you in a much stronger position soon after the discomfort is over.

Go ahead and ask the "dumb" question.

Volunteer to speak before the group regardless of how nervous you feel.

Initiate conversation with the other person standing by himself at the party.

Start learning a new skill even though you're lousy at first.

Wear that dress you like despite what others might think.

Decide you're going to accomplish something regardless of whether a little embarrassment or humiliation accompanies your actions. People aren't really paying much attention to you anyway. They're too concerned with their own image. Whatever discomfort you feel is only in your mind, not in others' minds.

*When you have a choice of being
right or being kind, be kind.*

• Wayne Dyer

Wayne Dyer was a professional speaker, author, and philosopher.

Being right may give you some immediate, short-term gratification. But proving rightness in an argument or heated debate can produce underlying side effects, which may become acutely painful down the road.

The most pronounced side effect: The other person or people you trumped aren't impressed with you. In fact, they may now put you in the jerk category.

But when you opt for kindness over rightness, you make the other person feel good about themselves. Which results in them having higher respect or affinity for you.

*If you can't be kind, at least
have the decency to be vague.*

• Steven Wright

꩜

Steven Wright is a comedian.

It's called tact. A skill that pays off immensely.

*It only takes a minute
to change your life.*

• Willie Jolley

Willie Jolley is a professional speaker and author.

Here's what can happen in 60 seconds or less:

You can make a decision. A decision that takes you in a particular direction, which in turn affects your entire life from that point forward.

Here's a good analogy. Upon entering the Ohio Turnpike south of Toledo, you have just a few seconds to decide whether to turn your steering wheel slightly to the left or slightly to the right. You make that decision, hold the wheel at about a 20-degree angle, and circle around one way or the other. If you chose West, in less than a minute you're headed to Chicago and beyond. If you chose East, in less than a minute you're headed to Cleveland and beyond. Two opposite journeys, with two opposite results — decided upon in less than a minute.

You can change your life in a big and better way by making a rather slight directional decision, then incrementally advancing in that direction from decision day forward. And the directional decision can be made in less than a minute.

Determine what outcome you want, evaluate your options, and make a directional decision. You really can change your life — or any aspect of it — in one enlightened minute.

Every man has enthusiasm at times.
One man has enthusiasm for thirty minutes,
another man has it for thirty days.
But it is the man who has it for thirty years
who makes a success in life.

• Edward B. Butler

Edward B. Butler was an entrepreneur. He lived from 1853 to 1928.

Your toughest challenge may very well be staying enthused — and continuing to put forth effort — even when no positive results are forthcoming.

Success, however you choose to measure it, comes in waves with peaks and troughs. And, or course, there are obstacles and setbacks along the way. The question is not whether or even when you will encounter difficult times (you will), but whether you're able to maintain your enthusiasm throughout.

Maintaining long-term enthusiasm doesn't mean you're enthusiastic all the time. It's normal for enthusiasm to rise and fall, rise and fall, rise and fall. The key is to be able to re-ignite your enthusiasm with some regularity. Shoot for a high average level of enthusiasm, not a constant state of it.

*It's been said that a pretty face
is a passport. But it's not true.
A pretty face is a visa,
and it runs out quickly.*

• Julie Burchill

Julie Burchill is a British writer.

It's also been said that you shouldn't judge a book by its cover, but that is exactly what people do.

Rightly or wrongly, people will form initial judgements about you based on how you come across. Tangible things like hair style, weight, and attire say things about you. So do intangibles like facial expression, body movement, and speech. Rightly or wrongly, such variables can open doors or cause doors to slam shut.

The good news here is twofold. First, almost all the variables are controllable. You can lose weight. You can get a more flattering hair style. You can dress better, even on a low budget. You can be more positive and congenial. You can improve your vocabulary. And don't tell me such changes wouldn't reflect "the real you." I'd like to think you're somewhat flexible, versatile, and always open to improvement.

As Julie alludes to however, your appearance or silver tongue won't get you very far if you can't back it up with performance. Have you ever known people who are all flash and no substance? They walk through a lot of open doors, but quickly fall through the trap door when their lack of contribution or productivity never materializes. This is the second piece of good news for you, assuming you're someone who can perform at a high level. In fact, if you look good and perform, you'll have more opportunities than you have time for.

Gardner: Why aren't you married?
Gable: No woman ever said yes.
Gardner: How many have you asked?
Gable: None.

• Clark Gable & Ava Gardner
in *Lone Star*

Clark Gable and Ava Gardner were movie actors.

Whether it's in love or business, if you don't ask, you don't get.

If you're afraid of getting a no, or being "rejected," then you may not ask. So the secret to getting is to have an effective way of handling the nos. May I offer you my method?

When I ask and someone says no, I know it's for one of four possible reasons:

- **The "fit" isn't right.** Whatever I'm asking for or proposing just doesn't fit into the other person's agenda or interest. If this is the case, I'm glad they said no. Otherwise, any deal we got into would be doomed from the start, and would be quite painful at that.
- **They're displaying bad judgement.** Remember, there's no accounting for poor taste. And I like people with good taste. I also like to deal with people who have vision; who can see the possibilities. So if they can't see a good idea when it's put right in front of their nose, I'm better off not dealing with them.
- **The timing isn't right.** They're interested, but are not ready to move on my proposal yet. Since timing affects everything, this doesn't bother me too much. I simply stay in touch and let the timing thing take care of itself.
- **They're not really in a position to say yes.** People (especially men) like to portray themselves as powerful, in authority, and well connected. But when put to the test, the truth comes out. They're not really in any sort of position to green-light much of anything.

Also, I try to have enough deals cooking at any given time so that I don't need any one of them. This lightens the sting of a no considerably.

An asset isn't an asset unless you use it.

• Michael Eisner

Michael Eisner is an entertainment executive.

I probably remind myself of this piece of wisdom at least once a month. You see, I am by nature a preserver. Like most people, I like to acquire things. But I often find myself preserving my possessions more than actually using them. Case in point: A year ago I bought a brand new set of deluxe screwdrivers to replace my old, beat up set. Whenever the need arose, however, I found myself still using the old ones. Evidently I was afraid of getting the new ones dirty or using them up.

But an asset isn't an asset unless you use it, I said to myself recently, as I initially grabbed an old screwdriver, then decided to use a new one instead.

What assets do you have that you're not using? Either use them, sell them off, or give them away so someone else can use them.

Do you have clothes that you never wear?

Do you have a computer, camera, or set of golf clubs that just collect dust?

Do you own a board game, old blanket, or set of dishes that sit idol?

Do you have an older car that rarely gets out of the garage?

What are you saving them for? An asset yearns to be used by someone, anyone.

What you think about, talk about,
and do something about, comes about.

• Larry Winget

❧

Larry Winget is a professional speaker and author.

This is the formula for attracting things into your life. If you think about it, talk about it, and do something about it, you will have it sooner or later.

Be clear about this, however: you need all three — think, talk, and do — to achieve results.

Some people just think; they never get past dreaming because they can't seem to verbalize what they have in mind or persuade anyone. Other people are really good talkers, but that's all they seem to do, talk. Only when you combine thinking and talking with actual roll-up-your-sleeves-and-get-your-hands-dirty work are you able to make it a reality.

*The name of the game is to stay
in the game. It's like poker —
if you can stay at the table,
you can win.*

• Richard Lord

Richard Lord is Richard Lord.

When I was a young man, I asked an older, seasoned salesperson what he attributed his success to. Without hesitation, he gave me a one-word answer: "longevity."

Longevity — or staying power — is crucial, without question. It may get rough out there on the field of play. But regardless of what happens, you must be able to hang in there if you are to win.

*You will never really be happy
or satisfied until you have found
a way to apply your unique human
capabilities to your life
and to your work.*

• Brian Tracy

Brian Tracy is a professional speaker and author.

You have some special talent, skill, or ability. (You may have even more than one.) Think about the ways you can utilize that special something throughout the course of your life.

Use it in your personal life in some way. Use it in your career or profession. Use it to serve others or better mankind in general. Just use it — or you may lose it. Do you know someone who has squandered their special gift? Don't be that person.

And if you find a way to monetize your talent or skill, you're really cooking. There's a market for almost every talent or skill. It's a matter of (a) identifying the market; the people who will pay for what you have, and (b) getting yourself in position to be paid.

Great spirits have always encountered violent opposition from mediocre minds.

• Albert Einstein

Albert Einstein was a theoretical physicist who lived from 1879 to 1955.

You can use violent opposition from people of mediocre minds to your advantage. Some people, for example, have adopted this stance: If everyone hates the idea, you know you're onto something.

There are a couple caveats, however.

The first: Overcoming violent opposition takes time. In the short run, the opposition may appear "correct," and can bury you if you lack staying power. In time, when your idea gains in popularity or acceptance, those who once lead the opposition may suddenly become a supporter, or even claim credit for mentoring you.

The second: Beware of the opposite — violent support from brilliant minds. When too many people like an idea, the idea is almost always seriously flawed and destined for trouble.

*Motivation always happens
in advance of something good,
not the other way around.*

• David Rich

❧

David Rich is a professional speaker and author.

Waiting for something to happen before you become motivated is like waiting until the room gets warm before lighting the fireplace. Since motivation precedes result, it's up to you to get motivated before the results show up.

Here are three ways to get yourself motivated:

- **Make something happen.** Instead of waiting for something to happen, make it happen. Divide your objectives into small, doable chunks and make one or two small ones happen. A succession of small accomplishments builds motivation and momentum.

- **Inhale motivating stimuli.** Read a book, listen to an audio program, talk to a friend, help a colleague, attend a seminar . . . whatever can fire you up is out there and available to you.

- **Cheerlead yourself.** Stand up, walk around, waive your arms, and talk to yourself in positive, forceful language. This is the mental equivalent of a physical workout. (In fact, you can physically workout and mentally workout at the same time.) See yourself as a persuasive leader that cheerleads others to perform at their best, and direct the same message to yourself.

One more thing. Stop depending on the acceptance or approval of other people to light your fire. If you wait for that, you've set yourself up to lose. Other people are focused on themselves, not on you. No one is going to follow you around all day and ply you with praise. The only person that can praise you as much as you deserve is you.

*The two most waisted days in the week
are yesterday and tomorrow.*

• Mike Ditka

Mike Ditka is a former football player, coach, and television commentator.

Do you spend time pondering the past? Activating the pangs of regret or re-living an ancient victory? Doing both can be instructional and enjoyable at times, I'll admit.

Do you spend time contemplating the future? Worrying about what will happen or planning for every possible contingency? Both are normal and we all do it.

Mentally time-traveling into your past or your future can be desirable at times. It only becomes a problem when you spend too much time with it. Then you're living in the past or the future and inadvertently squandering your present.

Only today — the here and now — contains the real power to create, to accomplish, to serve, and to enjoy. Focus the majority of your brain power on each day's activities; on what is happening right now. Your life will be more enjoyable and rewarding.

*Ninety percent of everything
that happens to you throughout your life
is due to your attitude, your words,
and your actions.*

• Rick Ott

Think of someone, either a famous person or otherwise, who accomplished something admirable. Now think of *how* that person accomplished it. No matter how it happened, you can trace it all back to their attitude, the words that came out of their mouth, and their actions.

You could also think of someone that caused great pain and suffering, and trace that back to their attitude, words, and actions, too.

Now think of your own life, including your accomplishments and your losses. How did all that happen? Does it go back to the same three variables — your attitude at the time, your words, and your actions?

What about other things that affect us? Things out of our control like circumstances, luck, timing, and other peoples' words and actions? All of that constitutes the other ten percent. Yes, there is a randomness element in the mix. But ninety percent of what happens to you is controllable by you, utilizing your three main tools: attitude, words, and actions.

The secret of happiness
is to count your blessings
while others are
adding up their troubles.

• William Penn

William Penn was a British entrepreneur and philosopher. He lived from 1644 to 1718.

There's a natural tendency for us to focus on our problems or what we don't have rather than on our good fortune and what we do have. This is not good. We should make a conscious effort to do exactly the opposite and appreciate what we do have and shrug off what we don't have.

Here's another perspective: We all have both good and bad aspects to our lives. You and I, for example, may have a different set of problems or good fortunes, but we both have a list of each regardless.

So while we're coveting another person's fortunes (perhaps even displaying envy, jealousy, or resentment), someone else is coveting your good fortunes with the same intensity. You have some wonderful things in your life, material and otherwise, that others wish they had. Why not focus on that and feel grateful and appreciative?

When you feel a wave of negativity overtaking you, switch your mental attention away from the desirable things you don't have and toward the wonderful things you do have. Tell yourself how grateful you are and how fortunate you feel. By doing so, you will . . .

- Be a much more pleasant person to be around.
- Reduce your tension and stress.
- Strengthen your mental state and thereby be better able to handle the various problems life tosses your way.
- Unleash your creative thinking.
- Attract even more good things into your life.
- Be a whole lot happier on a daily basis.

*You've got to be able to ride
the rollercoaster.
You've got to stay on track
when you're down,
knowing you're going to be
back up there.*

• Alice Cooper

❧

Alice Cooper is a rock star with several hit songs in the 1970s.

When you look closely at any successful person's life or career, you see that it is (or was) composed of numerous ups and downs. One of the contributing factors that makes a person successful is their ability to ride those ups and downs — especially the downs — without becoming victimized by the gyrations.

If you're in a down cycle now, you may be tempted to opt out. Quitting is only a good option when the up cycle, including all its spoils and rewards, just doesn't mean much to you. If, on the other hand, you have a passionate desire for the up, and/or you actually enjoy the journey, then you must hang in there. If you keep putting forth effort, you'll be up again.

If you're in an up cycle now, watch out. Don't become some wild n' crazy hedonist or you may just self-destruct (like way too many rock stars have done). Live conservatively, save money.

*There is no right or wrong,
there is only opinion.*

• Helen Slater
in *The Secret of My Success*

❧

Helen Slater is a movie actress.

Actually, there is right and wrong. It's just that everyone's definition of right and wrong is different.

Whatever you choose to believe you deem to be "right" (otherwise you wouldn't believe it), and if someone has a contrary belief they therefore must be "wrong."

You probably feel that certain other people believe wrong and do wrong . . . and you can bet there are people who think the same of you. Therefore, our collective rights and wrongs cancel out, leaving only opinion.

Do you ever find yourself striving to be deemed right and someone else wrong? To the point of even getting into a heated argument? Could it be you crave validation so much you'll say or do almost anything to show down someone else? Remember, when you go to such extremes to trump another, your image usually goes down, not up.

If, on the other hand, you want others to think highly of you, you might try validating their opinion once in a while.

*Whoever controls distribution
controls the deal.*

• Bill Brooks

Bill Brooks was a professional speaker and author.

This explains a lot.

It explains how Walmart, Home Depot, Costco, and other major retailers can make vendors grovel for a mere opportunity to pitch their goods to company buyers. Not to mention grinding those vendors down to the bone on cost, and dictating the terms and conditions.

Whoever controls distribution — which we'll define as direct access to the end buyer — will almost always have the upper hand. The rare exception happens only fleetingly. For example, a rock star, top athlete, or actor could be riding so high at a given point in time that they can gain the upper hand in negotiating with their label, team, or studio. But no one stays red hot forever, and when the artist or athlete inevitably cools down, the roles revert back to "normal," with the distributor back in the power position.

Understanding Bill's observation will serve you well. If you're the manufacturer, producer, athlete, or artist, you know from the start you must control your costs and accept the terms of the deal offered to you. (Of course, you will probably negotiate. Just don't overplay your hand.) It may also mean controlling some or all of the distribution yourself, if you're so inclined. (That's why Apple, Nike, Hanes, Ralph Lauren/Polo, and a host of other brands set up their own retail stores.)

If you want different results,
you have to do different things.

• Unknown

How many people do you know who want or expect things to turn out differently, yet they keep doing the same things day in and day out? Could the person in the mirror be guilty of the same behavior?

Perhaps it's time to shake things up a little; to suspend some of your routine activities and do things different for a while. Here are some possible ways to change:

- Instead of turning on the television this evening, read a new book (without the TV on in the background!).
- Instead of staying at home Friday evening, get out and do something.
- Instead of ordering the same menu item, try something you haven't had before (with less fat or sugar).
- Instead of calling on the same clients over and over, call on some new prospects a couple days a week.
- Instead of going to bed at 10pm every night, stay up 'till 1am working on some pet project.

Your biggest obstacle to a better lifestyle may very well be your own routine behavior. Think of it this way: Whatever you want to happen is not going to happen unless you do things differently from time to time. Is that time now?

If you show up and do your best,
it always turns out for the best,
no matter what happens.

• Bill Clinton

Bill Clinton served as the 42nd President of the United States.

The belief that however things turn out is really best for you is empowering. It can relieve you of tension and stress, anger and frustration, disappointment and regret. It can provide you with tremendous peace of mind, knowing that a different outcome, however attractive on the surface, wasn't really good for you after all.

There are two keys to this:

- **Different results are not necessarily bad results.** Just because things turn out differently than what you'd hoped for doesn't mean the result is any less valid. Many wonderful accomplishments came about by accident. Many people end up with a great spouse, a great career, or living in a great place — when none of that was part of their original plan.

- **You may have to improve on your "best."** While working on a home improvement project for a friend, she offered a brief criticism of my work. I instinctively replied "well, I'm doing my best." But as I continued to drip paint all over the walls and floor, a thought flashed in my mind. Maybe I'm not really doing as well as I could. Maybe my best can be better. So right then and there I gave it extra effort and improved my performance on the spot.

Give it your best — your new, improved best. Then accept whatever happens. Be happy and grateful for whatever happens, knowing it turned out for the best.

Friends come and go,
but enemies accumulate.

• Ben Stein

Ben Stein is a philosopher, author, and actor.

Be nice to people. Be respectful, too. And not to just the people in positions of power or authority.

In my 20s, I was an air personality at a radio station in Norfolk, Virginia. It was a Top 40 station with seven or eight of us "rock jocks" and only one newscaster. The news guy, an introverted fellow who worked by himself in a desolate corner of the building, was sort of the station's outcast. Once an hour he'd walk down the hallway into the news booth, do his three-minute newscast, then disappear back into his mouse hole. Except for an occasional "hey, how's it goin" mutterance, no one on the staff paid much attention to him.

Except me. Every once in a while I'd venture back into his little new-gathering room and strike up a conversation. We didn't talk about anything really substantive as I recall, but he did seem to enjoy the company.

Then one day the unexpected happened. Out of the blue, the owner of the station decided to change the format from Top 40 Rock to All News. And — get this — The Lone Newsguy was put in charge. He suddenly became everyone's boss!

Changing a radio station from rock to news is a 180-degree shift. As typically happens in such cases, the disc jockeys were all fired and a bunch of news people were hired. Except for me. The Lone Newsguy, who was now The Big Guy, not only asked me to stay on, but gave me a promotion. "Rick, you're the only person who ever talked to me," he said.

Do you inadvertently ignore the "little people" who cross your path day in and day out? People like the delivery person who brings packages, the IT person who fixes your equipment, or the hotel housekeeper who cleans your room? When you're nice to them, even in a small way, your travels through life will be a whole lot smoother than if you dis them.

When they say "I'll call you,"
it means you had better call them.

• Christine Dessimer

Christine Dessimer is a microbiologist and painter.

Whether it be in business or in relationships, know that the words "I'll call you," (or "I'll text you") are not to be taken at face value. Here's the translation: "I'll call you" means "If you want something to happen, you had better call me."

Why don't people just say something more accurate like "Call me next month and we'll discuss it further," or "We're not a good candidate for you," or "I've got a full schedule coming up, but the best time to reach me is Tuesday mornings"? That would be much more helpful, don't you think?

More than likely, when someone says "I'll call you" when they really have no intention to do so, they are (a) trying to end the present conversation and move on, and (b) really don't care much whether they re-connect with you again or not.

Whereas you do care. You're trying to get something going; trying to advance a relationship or make a sale. So . . . you'll end up having to call them — perhaps repeatedly — to get anywhere.

By the way, if you are guilty of saying one thing when you mean another thing, please stop. Do everyone a favor and say what you mean. Or, if you just can't bring yourself to speaking truthfully in such an instance, then the only other honorable thing to do is to provide the other person with the proper means to translate. As the words "I'll call you" slide out of your mouth, simultaneously hand them a copy of this book, opened to this page, and point here.

Cold-call selling is mostly a numbers game.
Referral selling is mostly a relationship game.
The numbers game will wear you down,
while the relationship game
will build you up.

• Bill Cates

Bill Cates is a professional speaker and author.

No wonder so many people come to dislike selling. They're wearing themselves out cold calling day in and day out. I think coal mining is an easier profession than cold calling strangers all day long.

Meanwhile, salespeople who concentrate on building relationships with qualified buyers, and asking them for referrals, seem to thrive on their daily activity. No wonder these salespeople succeed in the short run, build a solid sales career (or self-owned business) in the long run, and live a joyful life.

Beware of the opposite, however. Depending too much on your existing relationships and never cold calling new prospects can be a problem. Do a little cold calling with some regularity. Just make it a smaller percent of your effort, and make referral selling the larger percent.

Rick Ott

Rick Ott is a professional speaker, author, actor, money manager, graphic designer, and martial artist. He holds a B.A. in Advertising from Michigan State University, an M.B.A. from Virginia Commonwealth University, and a Black Belt from Grandmaster Dong's Martial Arts.

www.ingramcontent.com/pod-product-compliance
Lightning Source LLC
Chambersburg PA
CBHW071613040426
42452CB00008B/1333